Y0-CAD-372

Grade 6

Assessment Record Book

Making Meaning™

Developmental Studies Center™

2000 Embarcadero, Suite 305
Oakland, CA 94606

© 2003 Developmental Studies Center
All rights reserved.

The blackline masters in this publication are designed to be used with appropriate duplicating equipment to produce copies for classroom use only. Developmental Studies Center grants permission to classroom teachers to reproduce these masters.

Developmental Studies Center
2000 Embarcadero, Suite 305 • Oakland, CA 94606
510-533-0213 • 800-666-7270
www.devstu.org

ISBN 1-57621-419-2
Printed in Canada.

Assessment Overview

The *Assessment Record Book* is designed to help you make informed instructional decisions and track your students' reading comprehension and social development as you teach the *Making Meaning*™ lessons. The expectation in the *Making Meaning* program is that *all* of your students are developing at their own pace into readers with high levels of comprehension, and that they can all develop positive, effective interpersonal skills.

There are three types of assessments in the program: Social Skills Assessments, Class Comprehension Assessments, and Individual Comprehension Assessments. As you follow the lessons in the *Teacher's Manual*, an assessment box will alert you whenever one of these assessments is suggested. The assessment box will also direct you to the corresponding pages in the *Assessment Record Book*. Each kind of assessment is described briefly below.

SOCIAL SKILLS ASSESSMENT

The Social Skills Assessment (SSA) occurs at the end of Units 1, 5, and 7. This assessment allows you to note how well each student is learning and applying the social skills taught in the program. The SSA record sheet (pages 4–5) allows you to track how students are doing with particular skills over time. The assessment also allows you to track both overall participation in the lessons and how each student integrates the values of responsibility, respect, fairness, caring, and helpfulness into his behavior.

CLASS COMPREHENSION ASSESSMENT

The Class Comprehension Assessment (CCA) is a once-a-week assessment designed to help you assess the performance and needs of the whole class. The CCA usually occurs during guided or independent strategy practice lessons, at a time when the students would be using comprehension strategies they learned during the week. During a CCA, you have the opportunity to randomly observe students as they work in pairs or individually (selecting strong, average, and struggling readers) as you ask yourself key questions. Each week's CCA record sheet (see page 8) gives you space to record your thinking and provides suggestions for how to proceed based on your observations.

INDIVIDUAL COMPREHENSION ASSESSMENT

The Individual Comprehension Assessment (ICA) is an end-of-unit assessment designed to help you to assess the comprehension of individual students. The ICA helps you review each student's work and IDR conference notes to see how the students are using strategies and making sense of what they read. Each unit's ICA section (see pages 32–43) provides examples of student work for your reference. You can use the ICA Class Record Sheet (page 44) to track the students' progress over the year.

IDR CONFERENCE NOTES

Your notes from the IDR conferences you have with students are an important source of information for the ICA. While you do not need to document every IDR conference you have, it is important to document at least one conference per unit per student. Furthermore, at the end of Units 3 and 6, we suggest that you take a break from the lessons and devote a week to IDR. During this week you will have an opportunity to confer with every student and to document the conferences.

INFORMAL PORTFOLIO ASSESSMENT

We suggest that you create individual student folders to collect each student's IDR conference notes, filed chronologically. The *Student Book* and the folder comprise an informal portfolio which you can use to discuss the student's progress with the student or others. Before meeting with a student to discuss the portfolio, you might ask him to select one or two pieces of *Student Book* work that he feels are examples of good thinking he did while reading and be prepared to talk about this work.

Social Skills Assessment

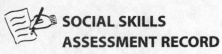

SOCIAL SKILLS ASSESSMENT RECORD
(UNITS 1, 5, AND 7)

Use the following rubric to score each student:

1 = does not implement
2 = implements with support
3 = implements independently

Participates in partner work and class discussions	UNIT 1										
	UNIT 5										
	UNIT 7										
Explains thinking and listens to others	UNIT 1										
	UNIT 5										
	UNIT 7										
Follows classroom procedures (e.g., moves to read-alouds and class meetings responsibly, observes class meeting ground rules, follows classroom library and independent reading procedures)	UNIT 1										
	UNIT 5										
	UNIT 7										
Uses "Turn to Your Partner" and "Think, Pair, Share" (e.g., faces partner, listens attentively, contributes ideas about the reading, question, or topic)	UNIT 1										
	UNIT 5										
	UNIT 7										
Acts on class norms	UNIT 1										
	UNIT 5										
	UNIT 7										
Is able to reflect on behavior	UNIT 1										
	UNIT 5										
	UNIT 7										
Takes responsibility for her learning and behavior	UNIT 1										
	UNIT 5										
	UNIT 7										
Reaches agreement with others	UNIT 5										
	UNIT 7										
Uses "Think, Pair, Write" (e.g., thinks quietly, shares with a partner, individually writes own thoughts)	UNIT 5										
	UNIT 7										
Uses prompts to add to others' thinking and to extend conversations	UNIT 5										
	UNIT 7										
Agrees and disagrees respectfully	UNIT 5										
	UNIT 7										
Confirms others' thinking by repeating back what she heard	UNIT 5										
	UNIT 7										
Asks clarifying questions	UNIT 5										
	UNIT 7										
Uses "Heads Together" (e.g., takes turns talking and listening in a group, contributes ideas about the reading, question, or topic)	UNIT 5										
	UNIT 7										
Includes others	UNIT 5										
	UNIT 7										
Gives reasons for opinions	UNIT 7										
Discusses opinions and gives feedback respectfully	UNIT 7										
Expresses true opinions	UNIT 7										
Supports others' independent work	UNIT 7										

	UNIT 1
	UNIT 5
	UNIT 7
	UNIT 1
	UNIT 5
	UNIT 7
	UNIT 1
	UNIT 5
	UNIT 7
	UNIT 1
	UNIT 5
	UNIT 7
	UNIT 1
	UNIT 5
	UNIT 7
	UNIT 1
	UNIT 5
	UNIT 7
	UNIT 1
	UNIT 5
	UNIT 7
	UNIT 5
	UNIT 7
	UNIT 5
	UNIT 7
	UNIT 5
	UNIT 7
	UNIT 5
	UNIT 7
	UNIT 5
	UNIT 7
	UNIT 5
	UNIT 7
	UNIT 7
	UNIT 7
	UNIT 7

Class
Comprehension
Assessment

Unit 2 ▸ Week 1

Exploring Expository Text: Text Structure

Observe the class and ask yourself:	All or most students	About half the students	Only a few students
▸ Do the students recognize expository text features?			
▸ Do they have a sense of what information a feature contributes?			

WHAT TO DO NOW:

▸ If *all or most students* are noticing expository text features and seem to have a sense of the information they contribute, proceed with Independent Strategy Practice on Day 4.

▸ If *about half the students* or *only a few students* are noticing expository text features and seem to have a sense of the information they contribute, you might want to repeat Days 1, 2, and 3 of this week using an alternative book before moving on to Day 4. Alternative books are listed in the Week 1 Overview.

Unit 2 ▸ Week 2

Exploring Expository Text: Questioning

Observe the class and ask yourself:	All or most students	About half the students	Only a few students
▸ Do the students understand the text?			
▸ Are they underlining sentences that address the questions?			

WHAT TO DO NOW:

▸ If **all or most students** are underlining passages that address the questions and showing evidence that they understand the text, proceed with Week 3.

▸ If **about half the students** are underlining passages that address the questions and showing evidence that they understand the text, proceed with Week 3 and plan to monitor the students who are having difficulty during independent reading. You might have them read a short passage from their book aloud to you and think of a question they could ask at that point in the reading. Then have them continue reading for a while and check in with them to see if their question was discussed.

▸ If **only a few students** are underlining passages that address the questions and are showing evidence that they understand the text, you might want to repeat this week using an alternative book before moving on. Alternative books are listed in the Week 2 Overview.

Unit 2 ▸ Week 3

Exploring Expository Text: Questioning

Observe the class and ask yourself:	All or most students	About half the students	Only a few students
▸ Are the students using their questions to guide their thinking about the text?			
▸ Are they referring to the text as they discuss their questions?			

WHAT TO DO NOW:

▸ If **all or most students** are using their questions to guide their thinking and referring to the text to talk about their questions, proceed with Unit 3.

▸ If **about half the students** or **only a few students** are using their questions to guide their thinking and referring to the text to talk about their questions, you might want to repeat this week using an alternative book before moving on to Unit 3. Alternative books are listed in the Week 3 Overview. Be aware that the students will have more opportunities to practice "Stop and Ask Questions" in the coming units.

Unit 3 ▸ Week 1

Analyzing Literature: Text Structure

Observe the class and ask yourself:	All or most students	About half the students	Only a few students
▸ Are the students inferring about the two characters, using clues from the text?			

WHAT TO DO NOW:

▸ If **all or most students** are inferring about the characters, using clues from the text, proceed with Day 4.

▸ If **about half the students** are inferring about the characters, using clues from the text, proceed with Day 4 and plan to check in with students who are having difficulty during IDR.

▸ If **only a few students** are inferring about the characters, using clues from the text, you might want to repeat Days 1, 2, and 3 of this week using an alternative book before moving on to Day 4. Alternative books are listed in the Week 1 Overview.

Unit 3 ▸ Week 2

Analyzing Literature: Questioning

Observe the class and ask yourself:	All or most students	About half the students	Only a few students
▸ Are the students using their questions to talk about their reading?			
▸ Are they referring to the text to discuss their questions?			

WHAT TO DO NOW:

▸ If *all or most students* are using questioning to understand and discuss their independent reading, proceed with Week 3.

▸ If *about half the students* or *only a few students* are using questioning to understand and discuss their independent reading, proceed with Week 3 (a repeat of Week 2) and monitor students who are having difficulty with questioning during IDR.

Unit 3 ▸ Week 3

Analyzing Literature: Questioning

Observe the class and ask yourself:	All or most students	About half the students	Only a few students
▶ Are the students using their questions to talk about their reading?			
▶ Are they referring to the text to discuss their questions?			

WHAT TO DO NOW:

▶ If **all or most students** are using questioning to understand and discuss their independent reading, proceed with Unit 4.

▶ If **about half the students** or **only a few students** are using questioning to understand and discuss their independent reading, repeat this week using an alternative book before moving on to Unit 4. Alternative books are listed in the Weeks 2 and 3 Overviews. Closely monitor and support students who are having difficulty by asking them questions during IDR and partner work, such as:

Q *What are you wondering about at this point in your reading?*

Q *What is a question you could ask at this point in the reading?*

Q *What question got you and your partner talking about the book?*

CLASS COMPREHENSION
ASSESSMENT RECORD

Unit 4 ▸ Week 1

Inference in Literature and Poetry

Observe the class and ask yourself:	All or most students	About half the students	Only a few students
▶ Are the students underlining passages that give clues about why the boy became afraid again?			
▶ Are they able to explain how these passages tell them why the boy became afraid?			

WHAT TO DO NOW:

▶ If *all or most students* are identifying clues about why **the boy became** afraid again, proceed with Independent Strategy Practice on Day 3.

▶ If *about half the students* or *only a few students* are identifying clues about why the boy became afraid again, consider repeating Days 1 and 2 of this week using an alternative book before moving on to Day 3. Alternative books are listed in the Week 1 Overview.

14 | Making Meaning™

Unit 4 ▸ Week 2

Inference in Literature and Poetry

Observe the class and ask yourself:	All or most students	About half the students	Only a few students
▸ Are the students able to identify lines in the poem that require an inference?			
▸ Are they able to make an appropriate inference for those lines?			

WHAT TO DO NOW:

▸ If **all or most students** are able to make inferences, proceed with Independent Strategy Practice on Day 4.

▸ If **about half the students** are able to make inferences, proceed with Day 4, but plan to monitor the students who are having difficulty with inferences during IDR by asking them questions such as:

Q *What is one thing that you know based on what you read today ?*

Q *Did the book tell you that directly, or did you figure it out from clues? What clues?*

▸ If **only a few students** are able to make inferences, consider repeating Days 1, 2, and 3 of this week using an alternative book before moving on to Day 4. Alternative books are listed in the Week 2 Overview.

**CLASS COMPREHENSION
ASSESSMENT RECORD**

Unit 4 ▸ Week 3

Inference in Literature and Poetry

Observe the class and ask yourself:	All or most students	About half the students	Only a few students
▸ Are the students able to describe what is happening in the poem?			
▸ Are their visualizations connected to the text?			
▸ Do they recognize clues that helped them visualize?			

WHAT TO DO NOW:

▸ If **all or most students** are able to make inferences and visualize what is happening in the poem, proceed with Independent Strategy Practice on Day 3.

▸ If **about half the students** or **only a few students** are able to make inferences and visualize what is happening in the poem, consider repeating Days 1 and 2 of this week using an alternative poem before moving on to Day 3. Alternative books are listed in the Week 3 Overview.

Unit 5 ▸ Week 1

Inferring About Causes and Effects

Observe the class and ask yourself:	All or most students	About half the students	Only a few students
▸ Are the students identifying clues about why Marianne gives Mrs. Book the feather?			

WHAT TO DO NOW:

▸ If **all or most students** are able to identify clues that explain why Marianne gives Mrs. Book the feather, proceed with Independent Strategy Practice on Day 4.

▸ If **about half the students** are able to identify clues that explain why Marianne gives Mrs. Book the feather, proceed with Day 4, but plan to check in with students who are having difficulty identifying simple causal relationships during IDR.

▸ If **only a few students** are able to identify clues that explain why Marianne gives Mrs. Book the feather, repeat Days 1, 2, and 3 of this week using an alternative book before moving on to Day 4. Alternative books are listed in the Week 1 Overview.

Unit 5 ▸ Week 2

Inferring About Causes and Effects

Observe the class and ask yourself:	All or most students	About half the students	Only a few students
▸ Are the students identifying clues about why Langston never felt like he had a home?			

WHAT TO DO NOW:

▸ If **all or most students** are able to identify clues that explain why Langston never felt like he had a home, proceed with Independent Strategy Practice on Day 4.

▸ If **about half the students** are able to identify clues that explain why Langston never felt like he had a home, proceed with Day 4, but plan to check in with students who are having difficulty identifying simple causal relationships during IDR.

▸ If **only a few students** are able to identify clues that explain why Langston never felt like he had a home, repeat Days 1, 2, and 3 of this week using an alternative book before moving on to Day 4. Alternative books are listed in the Week 2 Overview.

Unit 5 ▸ Week 3

Inferring About Causes and Effects

Observe the class and ask yourself:	All or most students	About half the students	Only a few students
▸ Are the students identifying clues about why whole forests were leveled by the eruption?			

WHAT TO DO NOW:

▸ If **all or most students** are able to identify clues in the excerpt about why whole forests were leveled by the eruption, proceed with Independent Strategy Practice on Day 4.

▸ If **about half the students** or **only a few students** are able to identify clues in the excerpt about why whole forests were leveled by the eruption, repeat Days 1, 2, and 3 of this week using an alternative book before moving on to Day 4. Alternative books are listed in the Week 3 Overview.

Unit 5 ▸ Week 4

Inferring About Causes and Effects

Observe the class and ask yourself:	All or most students	About half the students	Only a few students
▸ Are the students finding passages that describe relationships among the plants and animals?			
▸ Are they making sense of the excerpt?			

WHAT TO DO NOW:

▸ If *all or most students* are finding and understanding passages that describe relationships among the plants and animals, proceed with Unit 6.

▸ If *about half the students* or *only a few students* are finding and understanding passages that describe relationships among the plants and animals, repeat this week using an alternative book before moving on to Unit 6. Alternative books are listed in the Week 4 Overview.

Closely monitor the students who are having difficulty identifying cause and effect relationships during IDR by asking them questions such as:

Q *What is a* why *question you can ask about the part of the book you are reading right now?*

Q *Do you have any information so far that might help you answer that* why *question? If so, what information?*

Q *What do you think will happen as a result of [what the character is doing now]?*

Unit 6 ▸ Week 1

Exploring Important Ideas and Summarizing

Observe the class and ask yourself:	All or most students	About half the students	Only a few students
▶ Are the students able to identify an important idea in the passage?			
▶ Are they able to identify a supporting idea?			
▶ Is there evidence that they see the difference between important and supporting ideas in the passsage?			

WHAT TO DO NOW:

▶ If **all or most students** are able to identify and distinguish between important and supporting ideas, proceed with Week 2.

▶ If **about half the students** are able to identify and distinguish between important and supporting ideas, proceed with Week 2 and continue to closely observe the students who are not identifying and distinguishing these ideas. Many students will need repeated experiences to learn this complex skill.

▶ If **only a few students** are able to identify and distinguish between important and supporting ideas, repeat this week's lessons using an alternative book before moving on to Week 2. Alternative books are listed in the Week 1 Overview.

Unit 6 ▸ Week 2

Exploring Important Ideas and Summarizing

Observe the class and ask yourself:	*All or most students*	*About half the students*	*Only a few students*
▸ Are the students making reasonable distinctions between important and supporting information?			
▸ Are they supporting their thinking by referring to the story?			

WHAT TO DO NOW:

▸ If **all or most students** are making reasonable distinctions between important and supporting information and referring to the text to support their thinking, proceed with Week 3.

▸ If **about half the students** or **only a few students** are making reasonable distinctions between important and supporting information and referring to the text to support their thinking, you might want to repeat this week's lessons using an alternative book before moving on to Week 3. Alternative books are listed in the Week 2 Overview.

Unit 6 ▸ Week 3

Exploring Important Ideas and Summarizing

Observe the class and ask yourself:	All or most students	About half the students	Only a few students
▸ Are the students able to identify important information in the text?			
▸ Are they referring to the text to support their thinking?			

WHAT TO DO NOW:

▸ If *all or most students* are identifying important information and referring to the text to support their thinking, proceed with Day 4.

▸ If *about half the students* or *only a few students* are identifying important information and referring to the text to support their thinking, continue with the guided summarization lesson on Day 4, but plan to model writing the entire summary with the class. Then continue with Week 4, which is a repeat of Week 3. Closely monitor to see which students continue to have difficulty during Week 4.

Unit 6 ▸ Week 4

Exploring Important Ideas and Summarizing

Observe the class and ask yourself:	All or most students	About half the students	Only a few students
▶ Are the students able to identify important information in the text?			
▶ Are they referring to the text to support their thinking?			

WHAT TO DO NOW:

▶ If **all or most students** are identifying important information and referring to the text to support their thinking, proceed with Guided Strategy Practice on Day 4.

▶ If **about half the students** or **only a few students** are identifying important information and referring to the text to support their thinking, repeat the lessons in Week 3 again using an alternative book. Use the Teacher Notes in Week 3 to modify your instruction to support struggling students. Also support the students during IDR by asking them to identify important ideas and to verbally summarize what they have read.

Unit 6 ▸ Week 5

Exploring Important Ideas and Summarizing

Observe the class and ask yourself:	All or most students	About half the students	Only a few students
▸ Are the students able to identify important ideas in each section?			
▸ Can they summarize the information in a few sentences?			

WHAT TO DO NOW:

▸ If *all or most students* are able to identify important ideas in each section and summarize the information in a few sentences, proceed with Week 6.

▸ If *about half the students* or *only a few students* are able to identify important ideas in each section and summarize the information in a few sentences, bring the class together and summarize the remaining sections of the excerpt together, as you did in Steps 2 and 3 of today's lesson. Then plan to repeat the week using an alternative book before continuing with Week 6. Alternative books are listed in the Week 5 overview.

Unit 6 ▸ Week 6

Exploring Important Ideas and Summarizing

Observe the class and ask yourself:	All or most students	About half the students	Only a few students
▸ Do the students' summaries successfully communicate what their texts are about?			
▸ Is there evidence in the partners' feedback that they are understanding something about the texts being summarized?			
▸ Are the students revising or adding to their summaries based on the feedback?			

WHAT TO DO NOW:

▸ If **all or most students** are writing summaries that successfully communicate what their texts are about, continue with the Class Meeting on Day 4 and proceed with Unit 7.

▸ If **about half the students** are writing summaries that successfully communicate what their texts are about, collect the unsuccessful summaries, read them, and give feedback to the students. Have the students write second drafts based on your feedback (see the Teacher Note on Day 3, Step 3 of the lesson). Then continue with Unit 7.

▸ If **only a few students** are writing summaries that successfully communicate what their texts are about, do the Extension activity at the end of Week 5, Day 3. If you have already done the Extension once with the students' "Slower Than the Rest" summaries, do it again using photocopies of the students' own summaries from Week 6. Make sure to copy their summaries without their names. After analyzing the summaries in the Extension activity, have the students select another short text to summarize, and repeat Days 1, 2, and 3 of Week 6.

Unit 7 ▸ Week 1

Synthesizing

Observe the class and ask yourself:	All or most students	About half the students	Only a few students
▸ Can the students express an opinion about their reading?			
▸ Can they use information from the text to support their opinion?			

WHAT TO DO NOW:

▸ If **all or most students** are able to express and support an opinion about their reading, proceed with Week 2.

▸ If about **half the students** or **only a few students** are able to express and support an opinion about their reading, proceed with Week 2 and plan to check in with students who are having difficulty during the lessons and during their independent reading. Week 2 offers more experience with forming and writing about their opinions.

Unit 7 ▸ Week 2

Synthesizing

Observe the class and ask yourself:	*All or most students*	*About half the students*	*Only a few students*
▸ Can the students express an opinion about their reading?			
▸ Can they support their opinion with evidence from their text?			

WHAT TO DO NOW:

▸ If ***all or most students*** are able to express and support an opinion about their reading, proceed with the Class Meeting on Day 4.

▸ If ***about half the students*** or ***only a few students*** are able to express and support an opinion about their reading, repeat Day 3 of this week to provide additional experience with forming opinions about independent reading. Repeat Day 3 several times if necessary, then proceed with the Class Meeting on Day 4.

Unit 7 ▸ Week 3

Synthesizing

Observe the class and ask yourself:	All or most students	About half the students	Only a few students
▸ Are the students expressing their opinions about video games?			
▸ Are they supporting their opinions by referring to the article?			

WHAT TO DO NOW:

▸ If **all or most students** are able to consider the pros and cons of an argument and construct their own opinions, proceed with Day 3.

▸ If **about half the students** are able to consider the pros and cons of an argument and construct their own opinions, proceed with Day 3, but plan on checking in with students who are having difficulty during the whole-class discussion about "Sports Overload?" and during Independent Reading.

▸ If **only a few students** are able to consider the pros and cons of an argument and construct their own opinions, you might want to repeat Days 1 and 2 with an alternative article before continuing with Day 3. The article should present both the pros and cons of a topic or issue. Articles can be found on the Web sites listed as alternative sources on this week's Overview page.

Unit 7 ▸ Week 4

Synthesizing

Observe the class and ask yourself:	*All or most students*	*About half the students*	*Only a few students*
▸ *Are the students able to communicate what their book is about?*			
▸ *Do they support their recommendations by giving examples from the text? How?*			
▸ *Are they able to give and receive feedback in a helpful way?*			

WHAT TO DO NOW:

▸ If ***all or most students*** are able to communicate about their book and support their recommendations from the text, proceed with the Day 3.

▸ If ***about half the students*** or ***only a few students*** are able to communicate about their book and support their recommendations from the text, repeat this week of instruction using alternative book reviews. Alternative sources of book reviews are listed in the Week 4 Overview. Additionally, you might want to collect the students' book reviews, give feedback on them, and have the students write second drafts based on your feedback.

Individual
Comprehension
Assessment

Unit 2 ▶ Exploring Expository Text

The strategy-specific assessment helps you assess whether a student is able to use a strategy when prompted in a lesson. The ongoing comprehension assessment helps you assess her overall comprehension during IDR conferences. Be aware that a student may or may not use any particular strategy to make sense of her independent reading. The goal over time is for the students to be able to use appropriate strategies as needed to help them make sense of the texts they read independently.

STRATEGY-SPECIFIC ASSESSMENT

Review and consider for each student:

▶ Student work in Unit 2, including:
  • *Student Book,* pp. 4–11
  • *Student Book,* IDR Journal entries

As you analyze each student's work, ask yourself:

▶ *Does the student recognize and use text features and use questioning to make sense of expository texts?*

3 *Yes, most* of the student's work shows that she recognizes and uses text features and uses questioning to make sense of expository text.

2 *Some* of the student's work shows that she recognizes and uses text features and uses questioning to make sense of expository text.

1 *No, hardly any* of the student's work shows that she recognizes and uses text features and uses questioning to make sense of expository text.

ONGOING COMPREHENSION ASSESSMENT

Review and consider for each student:

▶ Your observations and impressions during IDR conferences in Unit 2.

Ask yourself:

▶ *Does this student show evidence that she is actively engaging with and making sense of text?*

3 *Yes, most* of my observations and impressions show evidence that she is actively engaging with and making sense of text.

2 *Some* of my observations and impressions show evidence that she is actively engaging with and making sense of text.

1 *No, hardly any* of my observations and impressions show evidence that she is actively engaging with and making sense of text.

Record your two assessment scores for each student on the ICA Class Record Sheet on page 44. Note that these scores denote the level of evidence *across* a student's work, rather than on any particular piece of work. Use the examples on the facing page as a benchmark for your assessments.

A student whose strategy-specific assessment would score a 3:

▶ Recognizes text features and has a sense of the information they contribute to the text.

▶ Uses questioning to help her think about and discuss a text.

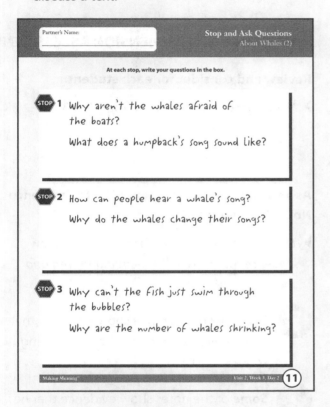

The goals are for students to recognize and use text features naturally to think about expository text and use questioning as needed to make sense of these texts. Students will be at different levels in learning to use these strategies. This is to be expected as students' sense-making processes develop over time with repeated reading experiences.

Continue to help the students practice by prompting them to demonstrate their use of these strategies in their independent reading.

A student whose ongoing comprehension assessment would score a 3:

▶ Describes what is happening in narrative texts she reads.

▶ Explains what she is learning from nonfiction or expository texts she reads.

▶ Notices when comprehension breaks down and stops to reread or question.

Unit 3 ▶ Analyzing Literature

The strategy-specific assessment helps you assess whether a student is able to use a strategy when prompted in a lesson. The ongoing comprehension assessment helps you assess his overall comprehension during IDR conferences. Be aware that a student may or may not use any particular strategy to make sense of his independent reading. The goal over time is for the students to be able to use appropriate strategies as needed to help them make sense of the texts they read independently.

STRATEGY-SPECIFIC ASSESSMENT

Review and consider for each student:

▶ Student work in Unit 3, including:

- *Student Book,* pp. 17–18

- *Student Book,* IDR Journal entries

As you analyze each student's work, ask yourself:

▶ *Does the student use questioning to make sense of narrative texts?*

3 *Yes, most* of the student's work shows evidence of using questioning to make sense of narrative text.

2 *Some* of the student's work shows evidence of using questioning to make sense of narrative text.

1 *No, hardly any* of the student's work shows evidence of using questioning to make sense of narrative text.

ONGOING COMPREHENSION ASSESSMENT

Review and consider for each student:

▶ Your IDR conference notes from Unit 3.

As you analyze each student's "IDR Conference Notes," ask yourself:

▶ *Do the conference notes for this student show evidence that he is actively engaging with and making sense of text?*

3 *Yes, most* of the notes show evidence that he is actively engaging with and making sense of text.

2 *Some* of the notes show evidence that he is actively engaging with and making sense of text.

1 *No, hardly any* of the notes show evidence that he is actively engaging with and making sense of text.

Record your two assessment scores for each student on the ICA Class Record Sheet on page 44 Note that these scores denote the level of evidence *across* a student's work, rather than on any particular piece of work. Use the examples on the facing page as a benchmark for your assessments.

A student whose strategy-specific assessment would score a 3:

▶ Generates relevant questions for a variety of texts.

▶ Uses his questions to discuss a text.

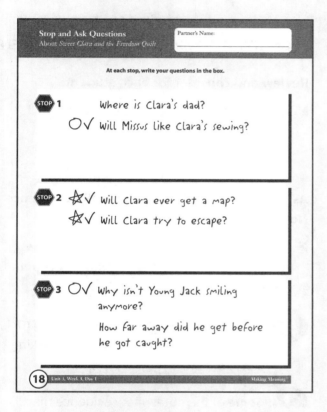

At this point in the program, some students may be able to use questioning only when prompted. This is to be expected. With time and practice, the students will learn to use questioning spontaneously and as needed to make sense of their independent reading. During IDR conferences, continue to encourage the students to talk about questions that come to mind and to use their questions to help them think about the text.

A student whose ongoing comprehension assessment would score a 3:

▶ Describes what is happening in narrative texts he reads.

▶ Explains what he is learning from nonfiction or expository texts he reads.

▶ Notices when comprehension breaks down and stops to reread or question.

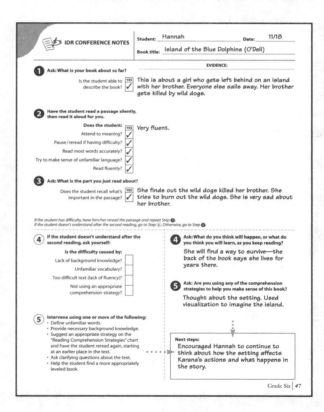

Unit 4 ▶ Inference in Literature and Poetry

The strategy-specific assessment helps you assess whether a student is able to use a strategy when prompted in a lesson. The ongoing comprehension assessment helps you assess her overall comprehension during IDR conferences. Be aware that a student may or may not use any particular strategy to make sense of her independent reading. The goal over time is for the students to be able to use appropriate strategies as needed to help them make sense of the texts they read independently.

STRATEGY-SPECIFIC ASSESSMENT

Review and consider for each student:

▶ Student work in Unit 4, including:

- *Student Book,* pp. 19–29

- *Student Book,* IDR Journal entries

As you analyze each student's work, ask yourself:

▶ *Does the student distinguish between explicit and implicit meanings in text and use inferences to make sense of poetry and narrative texts?*

3 **Yes, most** of the student's work shows evidence of using inferences to make sense of text.

2 **Some** of the student's work shows evidence of using inferences to make sense of text.

1 **No, hardly any** of the student's work show shows evidence of using inferences to make sense of text.

ONGOING COMPREHENSION ASSESSMENT

Review and consider for each student:

▶ Your IDR conference notes from Unit 4.

As you analyze each student's "IDR Conference Notes," ask yourself:

▶ *Do the conference notes for this student show evidence that she is actively engaging with and making sense of text?*

3 **Yes, most** of the notes show evidence that she is actively engaging with and making sense of text.

2 **Some** of the notes show evidence that she is actively engaging with and making sense of text.

1 **No, hardly any** of the notes show evidence that she is actively engaging with and making sense of text.

Record your two assessment scores for each student on the ICA Class Record Sheet on page 44. Note that these scores denote the level of evidence *across* a student's work, rather than on any particular piece of work. Use the examples on the facing page as a benchmark for your assessments.

A student whose strategy-specific assessment would score a 3:

▶ Describes what is happening in a variety of texts, including poems.

▶ Recognizes clues in poems and texts that can be used to make inferences.

▶ Describes inferences based on clues.

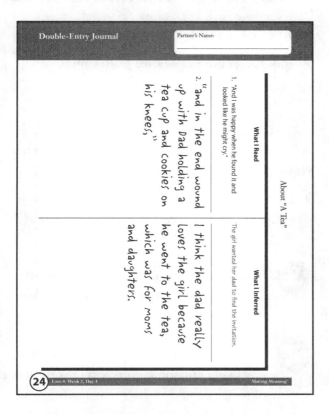

At this point in the program, some students may be able to make inferences only when prompted. During IDR conferences, continue to encourage these students to talk about what they know from their reading and the clues that helped them understand these things. As with all the strategies, the goal over time is for the students to be able to make inferences naturally and as appropriate as they read independently.

A student whose ongoing comprehension assessment would score a 3:

▶ Describes what is happening in narrative texts she reads.

▶ Explains what she is learning from nonfiction or expository texts she reads.

▶ Notices when comprehension breaks down and stops to reread or question.

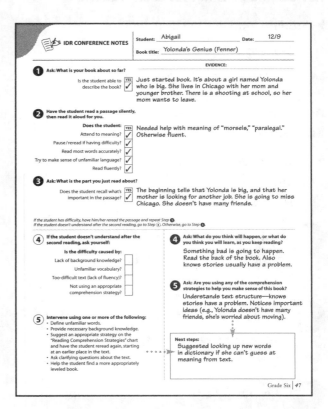

Unit 5 ▶ Inferring About Causes and Effects

The strategy-specific assessment helps you assess whether a student is able to use a strategy when prompted in a lesson. The ongoing comprehension assessment helps you assess his overall comprehension during IDR conferences. Be aware that a student may or may not use any particular strategy to make sense of his independent reading. The goal over time is for the students to be able to use appropriate strategies as needed to help them make sense of the texts they read independently.

STRATEGY-SPECIFIC ASSESSMENT

Review and consider for each student:

▶ Student work in Unit 5, including:

• *Student Book*, pp. 30–36

• *Student Book*, IDR Journal entries

As you analyze each student's work, ask yourself:

▶ *Does the student identify causes and effects in text?*

3 *Yes, most* of the student's work shows that he identifies causes and effects.

2 *Some* of the student's work shows that he identifies causes and effects.

1 *No, hardly any* of the student's work shows that he identifies causes and effects.

ONGOING COMPREHENSION ASSESSMENT

Review and consider for each student:

▶ Your IDR conference notes from Unit 5.

As you analyze each student's "IDR Conference Notes," ask yourself:

▶ *Do the conference notes for this student show evidence that he is actively engaging with and making sense of text?*

3 *Yes, most* of the notes show evidence that he is actively engaging with and making sense of text.

2 *Some* of the notes show evidence that he is actively engaging with and making sense of text.

1 *No, hardly any* of the notes show evidence that he is actively engaging with and making sense of text.

Record your two assessment scores for each student on the ICA Class Record Sheet on page 44. Note that these scores denote the level of evidence *across* a student's work, rather than on any particular piece of work. Use the examples on the facing page as a benchmark for your assessments.

A student whose strategy-specific assessment would score a 3:

▶ Uses clues in text to answer *why* and *what happens as a result* questions about a text.

▶ Describes how clues in text give information about causes and effects.

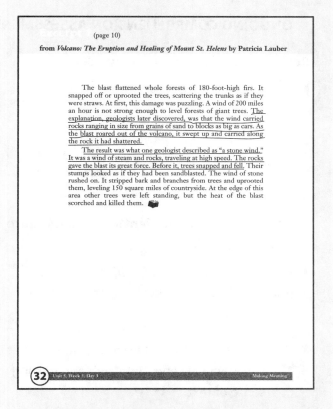

A student whose ongoing comprehension assessment would score a 3:

▶ Describes what is happening in narrative texts he reads.

▶ Explains what he is learning from nonfiction or expository texts he reads.

▶ Notices when comprehension breaks down and stops to reread or question.

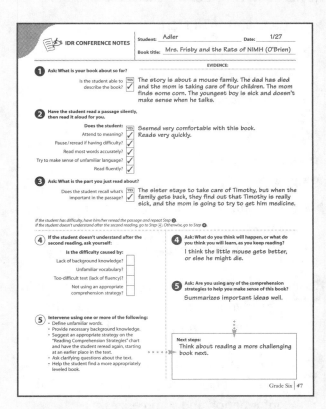

Identifying cause and effect relationships can be challenging and abstract for students. Many students may be able to identify these only when asked a *why* or *what happens as a result* question directly. The ability to identify these relationships develops with practice over time. During IDR conferences, continue to encourage the students to talk about the causes and effects they notice. This unit lays the foundations for more in-depth work with cause and effect in middle school.

INDIVIDUAL COMPREHENSION
ASSESSMENT (ICA)

Unit 6 ▶ Exploring Important Ideas and Summarizing

The strategy-specific assessment helps you assess whether a student is able to use a strategy when prompted in a lesson. The ongoing comprehension assessment helps you assess her overall comprehension during IDR conferences. Be aware that a student may or may not use any particular strategy to make sense of her independent reading. The goal over time is for the students to be able to use appropriate strategies as needed to help them make sense of the texts they read independently.

STRATEGY-SPECIFIC ASSESSMENT

Review and consider for each student:

▶ Student work in Unit 6, including:

- *Student Book,* pp. 37–48
- Written summary of "Slower Than the Rest" from Weeks 5 and 6.
- *Student Book,* IDR Journal entries

As you analyze each student's work, ask yourself:

▶ *Does the student identify important and supporting information and develop summaries from the important information?*

3 *Yes, most* of the student's work shows that she identifies important and supporting information and summarizes.

2 *Some* of the student's work shows that she identifies important and supporting information and summarizes.

1 *No, hardly any* of the student's work shows that she identifies important and supporting information and summarizes.

ONGOING COMPREHENSION ASSESSMENT

Review and consider for each student:

▶ Your IDR conference notes from Unit 6.

As you analyze each student's "IDR Conference Notes," ask yourself:

▶ *Do the conference notes for this student show evidence that she is actively engaging with and making sense of text?*

3 *Yes, most* of the notes show evidence that she is actively engaging with and making sense of text.

2 *Some* of the notes show evidence that she is actively engaging with and making sense of text.

1 *No, hardly any* of the notes show evidence that she is actively engaging with and making sense of text.

Record your two assessment scores for each student on the ICA Class Record Sheet on page 44. Note that these scores denote the level of evidence *across* a student's work, rather than on any particular piece of work. Use the examples on the facing page as a benchmark for your assessments.

A student whose strategy-specific assessment would score a 3:

▶ Distinguishes between important and supporting ideas in texts.

▶ Refers to text to explain how information supports important ideas.

▶ Uses important ideas to summarize a text.

Summary of "Slower Than the Rest"

      This is a short story about a boy named Leo and his turtle. Everybody thinks Leo is slow because he isn't good in school. He's pretty lonely until the turtle becomes his best friend. Leo shares his turtle at school to explain how forest fires can hurt slower animals, and the class likes Leo's report. He gets an award for his presentation and feels very happy at the end of the story.

Working with summarization and important ideas in Grade 6 lays the foundation for continued work in these areas in later grades. Distinguishing between important and supporting ideas is a complex skill that develops with repeated experiences over time. Some students may continue to need support in determining important ideas and summarizing at the end of this unit.

A student whose ongoing comprehension assessment would score a 3:

▶ Describes what is happening in narrative texts she reads.

▶ Explains what she is learning from nonfiction or expository texts she reads.

▶ Notices when comprehension breaks down and stops to reread or question.

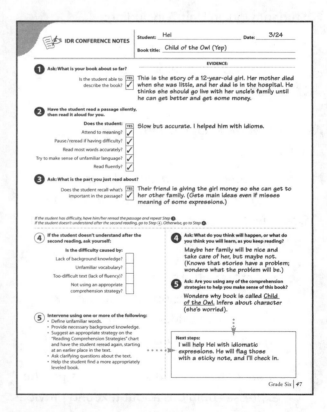

IDR CONFERENCE NOTES

Student: Hei   Date: 3/24

Book title: Child of the Owl (Yep)

EVIDENCE:

1 Ask: What is your book about so far?

Is the student able to describe the book? [YES ✓] This is the story of a 12-year-old girl. Her mother died when she was little, and her dad is in the hospital. He thinks she should go live with her uncle's family until he can get better and get some money.

2 Have the student read a passage silently, then read it aloud for you.

Does the student: [YES] Slow but accurate. I helped him with idioms.
Attend to meaning? ✓
Pause/reread if having difficulty? ✓
Read most words accurately? ✓
Try to make sense of unfamiliar language? ✓
Read fluently? ✓

3 Ask: What is the part you just read about?

Does the student recall what's important in the passage? [YES ✓] Their friend is giving the girl money so she can get to her other family. (Gets main ideas even if misses meaning of some expressions.)

If the student has difficulty, have him/her reread the passage and repeat Step ③.
If the student doesn't understand after the second reading, go to Step ④. Otherwise, go to Step ⑤.

4 If the student doesn't understand after the second reading, ask yourself:

Is the difficulty caused by:

Lack of background knowledge? ☐
Unfamiliar vocabulary? ☐
Too-difficult text (lack of fluency)? ☐
Not using an appropriate comprehension strategy? ☐

5 Intervene using one or more of the following:
• Define unfamiliar words.
• Provide necessary background knowledge.
• Suggest an appropriate strategy on the "Reading Comprehension Strategies" chart and have the student reread again, starting at an earlier place in the text.
• Ask clarifying questions about the text.
• Help the student find a more appropriately leveled book.

④ Ask: What do you think will happen, or what do you think you will learn, as you keep reading?

Maybe her family will be nice and take care of her, but maybe not. (Knows that stories have a problem; wonders what the problem will be.)

⑤ Ask: Are you using any of the comprehension strategies to help you make sense of this book?

Wonders why book is called Child of the Owl. Infers about character (she's worried).

Next steps:
I will help Hei with idiomatic expressions. He will flag those with a sticky note, and I'll check in.

Grade Six | 47

Unit 7 ▶ Synthesizing

The strategy-specific assessment helps you assess whether a student is able to use a strategy when prompted in a lesson. The ongoing comprehension assessment helps you assess his overall comprehension during IDR conferences. Be aware that a student may or may not use any particular strategy to make sense of his independent reading. The goal over time is for the students to be able to use appropriate strategies as needed to help them make sense of the texts they read independently.

STRATEGY-SPECIFIC ASSESSMENT

Review and consider for each student:

▶ Student work in Unit 7, including:

- *Student Book,* pp. 49–57
- Students' written summaries and reviews
- *Student Book,* IDR Journal entries

As you analyze each student's work, ask yourself:

▶ *Does the student summarize and express opinions about texts, both orally and in writing? Does the student provide evidence from texts to support his opinions?*

3 *Yes, most* of the student's work shows that he expresses opinions about text and provides evidence from text to support his opinions.

2 *Some* of the student's work shows that he expresses opinions about text and provides evidence from text to support his opinions.

1 *No, hardly any* of the student's work shows that he expresses opinions about text and provides evidence from text to support his opinions.

ONGOING COMPREHENSION ASSESSMENT

Review and consider for each student:

▶ Your IDR conference notes from Unit 7.

As you analyze each student's "IDR Conference Notes," ask yourself:

▶ *Do the conference notes for this student show evidence that he is actively engaging with and making sense of text?*

3 *Yes, most* of the notes show evidence that he is actively engaging with and making sense of text.

2 *Some* of the notes show evidence that he is actively engaging with and making sense of text.

1 *No, hardly any* of the notes show evidence that he is actively engaging with and making sense of text.

Record your two assessment scores for each student on the ICA Class Record Sheet on page 44. Note that these scores denote the level of evidence *across* a student's work, rather than on any particular piece of work. Use the examples on the facing page as a benchmark for your assessments.

A student whose strategy-specific assessment would score a 3:

▸ Summarizes from important ideas in a text.

▸ Forms opinions and refers to the text to support his opinions.

▸ Communicates effectively to others about what a text is about and his opinion of it.

Review of Island of the Blue Dolphins
by Scott O'Dell
Reviewed by Drake Frisbie

This story is about a young girl named Karana who has to survive alone on an island. All of the other people that lived on the island leave on a ship. As the ship is leaving, Karana notices that her brother is still on the island. She goes back to get him, but they both get left behind. When her brother is killed by wild dogs, Karana is left completely alone. The rest of the book tells how she survives.

I recommend this book because it is an adventure story about how a girl survives alone in nature. You might think the story is not believable, but it is actually based on a true story. It's easy to imagine how scary it would be to be left alone. Karana is inspiring because she is so brave no matter what happens. You will remember Island of the Blue Dolphins for years and years after you read it.

Synthesizing can be a challenging comprehension strategy for students to learn and integrate into their reading. The synthesis work in this unit lays the foundation for continued work with the strategy in later grades.

A student whose ongoing comprehension assessment would score a 3:

▸ Describes what is happening in narrative texts he reads.

▸ Explains what he is learning from nonfiction or expository texts he reads.

▸ Notices when comprehension breaks down and stops to reread or question.

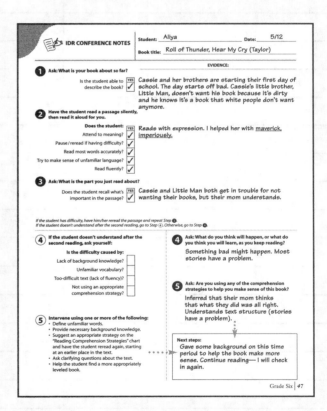

IDR CONFERENCE NOTES

Student: Aliya   Date: 5/12

Book title: Roll of Thunder, Hear My Cry (Taylor)

EVIDENCE:

1 Ask: What is your book about so far?

Is the student able to describe the book? [YES ✓]   Cassie and her brothers are starting their first day of school. The day starts off bad. Cassie's little brother, Little Man, doesn't want his book because it's dirty and he knows it's a book that white people don't want anymore.

2 Have the student read a passage silently, then read it aloud for you.

Does the student:
Attend to meaning? [YES ✓]   Reads with expression. I helped her with maverick, imperiously.
Pause/reread if having difficulty? ✓
Read most words accurately? ✓
Try to make sense of unfamiliar language? ✓
Read fluently? ✓

3 Ask: What is the part you just read about?

Does the student recall what's important in the passage? [YES ✓]   Cassie and Little Man both get in trouble for not wanting their books, but their mom understands.

If the student has difficulty, have him/her reread the passage and repeat Step 3.
If the student doesn't understand after the second reading, go to Step 4. Otherwise, go to Step 4.

4 If the student doesn't understand after the second reading, ask yourself:

Is the difficulty caused by:
Lack of background knowledge? ☐
Unfamiliar vocabulary? ☐
Too-difficult text (lack of fluency)? ☐
Not using an appropriate comprehension strategy? ☐

5 Intervene using one or more of the following:
· Define unfamiliar words.
· Provide necessary background knowledge.
· Suggest an appropriate strategy on the "Reading Comprehension Strategies" chart and have the student reread again, starting at an earlier place in the text.
· Ask clarifying questions about the text.
· Help the student find a more appropriately leveled book.

4 Ask: What do you think will happen, or what do you think you will learn, as you keep reading?
Something bad might happen. Most stories have a problem.

5 Ask: Are you using any of the comprehension strategies to help you make sense of this book?
Inferred that their mom thinks that what they did was all right. Understands text structure (stories have a problem).

Next steps:
Gave some background on this time period to help the book make more sense. Continue reading— I will check in again.

Grade Six | 47

INDIVIDUAL COMPREHENSION ASSESSMENT
CLASS RECORD SHEET

STUDENT NAMES	UNIT 2	UNIT 3	UNIT 4	UNIT 5	UNIT 6	UNIT 7

IDR Blackline Masters

Questions you can ask to probe student thinking:

▶ *What did you think about when you chose to read this book?*

▶ *What have you written in your Reading Log about this book?*

▶ *What reading comprehension strategy might you use when you go back to this book?*

▶ *What reading goals do you have? What do you think you need to work on?*

Genre-specific questions you can ask:

FICTION

▶ *What is this story about?*

▶ *What is the plot (or what happens) in this story?*

▶ *(Read the information on the back cover.) What have you found out about that so far?*

▶ *What have you inferred about the character(s)? What problem(s) do they face?*

▶ *Is the setting important in this story? Why do you think so?*

▶ *What part have you found interesting or surprising? Why?*

▶ *What are you wondering about?*

▶ *What do you visualize (see/hear/feel) as you read these words?*

▶ *What do you think the author means by _____?*

▶ *What do you think will happen in the coming pages?*

NONFICTION/EXPOSITORY

▶ *What is this book about?*

▶ *Summarize what you've read so far.*

▶ *(Read the information on the back cover.) What have you found out about that so far?*

▶ *(Look at the table of contents.) What do you think you will find out about _____ in this book?*

▶ *What's something interesting or important about what you've read so far?*

▶ *Is the author giving facts or opinions here? How do you know?*

▶ *What are you wondering about?*

▶ *What do you expect to learn about as you continue to read?*

▶ *What information does this [diagram/table/graph/other text feature] give you?*

POETRY

▶ *What is this poem about?*

▶ *What do you visualize (see/hear/feel) as you read these words?*

▶ *What do you think the poet means by _____?*

▶ *What can you infer from the line(s) _____?*

Self-monitoring strategies you can teach one-on-one:

☐ *Use clues from surrounding words to try to figure out what something means.*

☐ *Look up unfamiliar words in the dictionary, or ask someone.*

☐ *Stop and reread when confused.*

☐ *Stop and ask a question when confused, then reread.*

☐ *Stop at the end of difficult paragraphs, review, and summarize quietly before continuing.*

☐ *Make notes about important ideas from a book in your IDR Journal. Review the notes before and as you continue reading the book.*

IDR CONFERENCE NOTES

Student: _____ **Date:** _____

Book title: _____

EVIDENCE:

1 **Ask: What is your book about so far?**

Is the student able to describe the book? | YES | ☐

2 **Have the student read a passage silently, then read it aloud for you.**

Does the student: | YES

Attend to meaning? ☐

Pause/reread if having difficulty? ☐

Read most words accurately? ☐

Try to make sense of unfamiliar language? ☐

Read fluently? ☐

3 **Ask: What is the part you just read about?**

Does the student recall what's important in the passage? | YES | ☐

If the student has difficulty, have him/her reread the passage and repeat Step ❸.
If the student doesn't understand after the second reading, go to Step ④. Otherwise, go to Step ④.

4 **If the student doesn't understand after the second reading, ask yourself:**

Is the difficulty caused by:

Lack of background knowledge? ☐

Unfamiliar vocabulary? ☐

Too-difficult text (lack of fluency)? ☐

Not using an appropriate comprehension strategy? ☐

4 **Ask: What do you think will happen, or what do you think you will learn, as you keep reading?**

5 **Ask: Are you using any of the comprehension strategies to help you make sense of this book?**

5 **Intervene using one or more of the following:**
• Define unfamiliar words.
• Provide necessary background knowledge.
• Suggest an appropriate strategy on the "Reading Comprehension Strategies" chart and have the student reread again, starting at an earlier place in the text.
• Ask clarifying questions about the text.
• Help the student find a more appropriately leveled book.

Next steps: